Never Needed Saving

Essays and Stories

Heather Leigh Williams

Least Shining Crescent Press

Least Shining Crescent Press
Cambridge, Massachusetts, USA

www.leastshiningcrescent.com

Copyright © Heather Leigh Williams, 2009
All rights reserved.

ISBN 978-0-578-03285-6

Least Shining Crescent Press publishes unique books expressive of life in all its glory. Consult our website (www.leastshiningcrescent.com) for more information.

For inquiries or whatever contact us by email:
leastshiningcrescent@gmail.com.

Contents

Introduction	1
A Storm is Coming	3
You Had My Great Grandbaby Yet?	9
Dig Cuss Sleep	21
Counting Crows	27
Goodbye to Uncle Tom	33
Sarah Heartburn Runs Away	37
About the Author	46
Also from Least Shining Crescent Press	47

Introduction

If you want to die rich, get to know Heather Williams as a friend. If you want to die laughing, read what Heather Williams writes. If you don't want to die at all and just live forever, Heather can't help you there, but she makes an excellent friend who writes well, and does a great impersonation of her grandmother.

Tom Jester

A Storm is Coming

A storm is coming. Wind is howling. Wind chimes banging. Acorns pelting the house and deck. I can't sleep. Took a bath. Drinking a second beer and soon a third. Read my book for a while. Seems the brewing storm has peaked something in me and refuses to let me sleep tonight.

On the way to Gastonia, I thought of Grandma and how she has, all my life, loved me so dearly, without reservation, often in my mind without good reason to and wondering what in the world I had done to deserve her devotion. She told me a long time ago that the first time she laid eyes on me, when I was just a babe-in-arms, she knew we understood each other. And how I was her "pet", coming from anyone else I'd hate it but from her, it was an honor. What a lucky life to have had her as my champion.

I miss her now. She spends her days 70 years in the past with loved ones long since gone. She is a young woman again in North Carolina surrounded by her aunts and cousins and her grandmother. I walked the streets

Never Needed Saving

she walked and smelled tea olives all around me but never found the shrub. I wondered if they bloomed for Grandma back those long years ago.

I visited the graves of her mother and dad and felt her sense of longing for them. I brushed the dirt and debris off her dad's grave marker. It's been so long since she's seen them, smelled them, touched them, heard them. How can I cling to her? She is 96, house bound, blind, confused. She is provoked with herself for not learning Braille because she certainly did not expect to live this long and she misses books. She misses writing letters. Her gums are so tired her teeth just slide out of socket into her hand while eating. There is no pain; her gums simply let go. She and Granddaddy have super slow motion walker collisions-head on. They both hit the ground and have to wait for someone to help them get up. Some days, she thinks her son, my father, is her long gone brother. She thinks her Aunt Mabel is in a North Carolina hospital alone, with no hands.

Yet, she still remembers me. She knows my voice when I call. I call her often. So I can tell her how much I love her one more time. Just in case. I tell her I want her to remember the love I feel for her and how grateful I am to her. She promises me she will. How we are together, always. Nothing can keep us apart. I tell her how she saved me. She says I never needed saving. I try and beg to differ but she says "No, Girly, you never have needed saving. Maybe you just needed reminded of that. And I am happy to be the one to remind you." She still calls me "Girly" and tells me how she loves me so. She doesn't know my children or why I am in Tennessee but she still knows me. She threatens to get in her car and drive to see me.

Never Needed Saving

Lately, I can't get her off of my mind. I am 40 years old and I don't know how I will fill the void that her leaving will create in me. Nowadays, I call Elle, her friends and my sister "Girly." I talk in Grandma's voice to offer solace to myself and to practice because like a friend said to me last week "When she is gone, you'll be left with her voice. And Heather, that is something, you know." Liked to killed me.

I am selfish and greedy for her. I want her back. I want to sit next to her in church and hold her hand. I want her to offer me a peppermint when I start fidgeting because church bored the nightmares out of me then and still does now. She used to encourage me to attend church. When I told her I felt the presence of the Divine in the dark of a desert morning with a billion stars shining and the Milky Way lazing above me and thousands of bats returning home, she allowed that. When I told her the feel of dirt between my fingers kept me humble, she believed me. She didn't try to make me want church anymore. She understood I need to be outside of manmade walls to feel the Great Big Love, she said that's alright, God understands souls like me. Glad to hear someone other than her does.

I want to smell her Sensodyne and Sanka breath when she talks close to me and asks me what's really bothering me and reminds me that I don't have to pretend with her, my tears won't upset her one bit and it's best if I let them out and let them go. I miss walking into her house and calling her name and her calling back "Wooooohoo!" from her bedroom telling me to come see her she's just putting her stockings on. I want to eat Campbell's Tomato soup, crackers and Oleo with her. I want to see her with her hat and driving gloves on ready

Never Needed Saving

to have her 62 hairs set at the Penney's hair salon. I want another letter from her in her precise script telling me about a trip she took to Minnesota or Paris or Panama.

I am greedy for more of her. How can I have so much greed for her and at the same time want her to feel the unencumbered feeling that, hopefully, Elsewhere offers? The thought of her being Elsewhere seems unbearable to me. Elsewhere. Maybe these visits she's been having are her loved ones beckoning to her to come on over, the water's fine. Maybe they are enticing her with memories until her will, like her gums, just decides to let go. I don't know anything. I don't know how it works.

Do the ones we leave behind when we are born mourn us the way we mourn the ones who die, leaving us for Elsewhere? I wonder this all the time these days.

I know one thing. She taught me what Love is. It is absolute and shining. Nothing can diminish the glow. Not Time, not dementia, not distance, not death. And still Elsewhere seems so very far away. I can feel her going a little bit more each day. Some days, she's too tired to get out of bed when I call. Once, not long ago I asked her to please, when she goes, will she please come see me one last time before she's off to Neverland? She said she would if she could. She said not even death will part us, it'll just seem to but I'm not to be misled. "Ooooo, girly, don't you worry even a bit. I'll always be with you." And now, I tell her the same. The last time we talked I told her that I'll carry her with me all the days of my life. And that it was she who taught me to be gentle. It was she who taught me to listen. It was she who taught me patience. It was she who encouraged me to write. It was she who told me not to worry one bit what others may

Never Needed Saving

think--"Now, you know what I mean, Heather, I've worried too much and it kept me from doing what was right and true for me. Don't say it until you know it is true then keep your chin up and mark my words, it will turn out better than you ever imagined. Be brave, girly. And you teach your chirren to listen to their hearts. They'll never be led astray. Teach them to trust themselves. That's all you have to do. Remind them. The rest is just simple rules like grammar or arithmetic. Basic things. Remind them that they already know."

Shawn Mullins sings a song called Shimmer. The chorus goes like this:

> I want to shimmer.
>
> I want to shine.
>
> I want to radiate.
>
> I want to live.
>
> I want to love. I want to try and learn how not to hate.

We're born to shimmer, we're born to shine. We're born to radiate. We're born to live. We're born to love.

We're born to never hate.

And I can't get that song out of my head tonight, rather this early early morning.

And now the storm has passed leaving behind a gentle much needed rain. I'm on the porch, rockin in the chair listening to the horse nicker at me in the dark. All cried out and my load is lighter. If you've read all this, I thank you.

The rain sounds too good to go to sleep.

Never Needed Saving

You Had My Great Grandbaby Yet?

My due date found me disgruntled, weepy and trying to sit on my head the way Mork used to on Mork and Mindy. I could not do it. My belly was 40 weeks full. It was my last attempt at finding a comfortable position. All others had failed. The phone rang. And rang. Finally, on the seventh ring, I picked it up and said Hello.

"This is Frances' secretary calling for her granddaughter. Hedder Marie, is that you?"

Grandma's failing eyesight forced her to depend on Granddaddy to dial the phone for her. She disapproved of his nickname for me and how his phone conversations often veered to what she deemed inappropriate for polite company.

"Hi Granddaddy."

"You had my great grandbaby yet?"

"No sir, I have not. I'm pretty sure I never will."

"Hmm. Sounds like you are like Momma was. She kept 'em safe and sound until they practically fell out of her. 'Course all 11 of us were born at home, all of us had

Never Needed Saving

enormous noggins. I'll bet this baby has a huge head, too. Your great Aunt Fannie weighed 16 lbs. when she was born. That was in 1899 and Momma passed her just fine. But Momma was built for big babies and you aren't so you might not want to follow her example of 11 children. She just couldn't keep her legs closed! She was a passionate woman, yes, a very passionate woman."

Jesus Christ. As disturbing as the mental picture of my great grandmother with her legs perpetually spread, it was less disturbing than his talk of monstrous baby heads.

"Umm. Wow, Granddaddy. I don't think I can handle this conversation today." This only encouraged him to continue.

"Nothin' to be embarrassed about! You come from a long line of hot-blooded women and none of us would be here if they hadn't been willing to open their legs. Uh-oh."

I heard Grandma in the background decidedly provoked with him.

"Grainger Williams! What are you saying?! You stop talking like that! I declare. Is that Heather? Give me that phone now, please."

Granddaddy was chuckling. He told me to be good and Grandma came on the phone.

"Oh, Heather, he is incorrigible! Terrible. Now, girly, tell me how you are. Are you all right?"

I told her I was a little tired but fine. But I wasn't fine. I couldn't sleep, walk, sit, breathe, stand or lie down. For the past two weeks, a small stranger's foot had been permanently lodged in the left side of my rib cage. For months, she rolled like a dolphin, playful and serene, in

Never Needed Saving

the center of me. I would sit up in the dark of night with my hands on my belly feeling her rolling and rolling around. She no longer had room for such lollygagging. I should've wanted my mother with me but I'd felt a guilty relief when Mom told me she wouldn't be able to come up from Florida to be with me. I wanted Grandma with me.

"You certainly don't sound fine, girly. Tell me."

"The doctor lies to me, the midwife lies to me. They said I'd pass a mucous plug. I haven't. I've been looking and looking."

I had not asked for a specific description of the mucous plug. My mind had immediately gone to a smaller, more viscous version of the Mr. Stop-O-Fart that my brother, Grainger had given to me for Christmas a few years before. It was shaped like a wooden Hope Diamond and it had obviously been a plug. I'd stopped listening a precisely the moment pertinent plug information was being given to me by the doctor. For the last week, I had spent hours in the bathroom looking in earnest for this mysterious, labor-is-imminent-plug. My vagina had developed symptoms of a very slight cold. Mucous, yes, plug, no.

"Heather, what did you say? A mucous plug from your va-, never mind. Have you had a B.M.?" I was surprised she'd said that first syllable of the word vagina. A lady does not say 'vagina'. I was not surprised to hear her inquiring about my bowel activity. It was her favorite diagnostic question. When presented with a grandchild feeling poorly. I could tell her that my throat hurt or I was covered in poison ivy or I had a terrible hangnail-didn't matter, she needed to know when my bowels had last moved.

Never Needed Saving

"No, Grandma, I have not had a B.M. The only things coming out of me are urine and tears."

"Well, I think you need to have a B.M. Ask your doctor if she'll give you an enema or maybe some castor oil." No and no. In the background, I heard Granddaddy beg to differ.

"What she needs, Frances, is to have my great granddaughter." She hushed him up.

"Grandma, he's right. Only I need to tell you a secret. I have been thinking and I am not sure that I even like children. I only baby-sat for the money." And to make out with boys, if I was lucky.

"Furthermore, Grandma, I should have been reading all these parenting books but I haven't. I've read Kahlil Gibran and only the beginning of Dr. Spock's book. You know the very, very beginning where he says 'Trust yourself. You know more than you think you do.' The birthing class instructor drives me crazy. She has five kids. She is still breastfeeding her youngest. He is six years old. She says her boys never have strep throat or colds. She is convinced nursing her kids until they have to sign up for the Selective Service is the reason."

She had also convinced the idiot in the class, me, that in order to have a healthy baby we must eat a minimum of 100 grams of protein per day. I faithfully did this and gained pretty close to 1 billion pounds. She and the doctor, midwife had all tried to convince me I would indeed know when I was in labor. I assured them I would not. They had all told me I would pass the elusive mucous plug. I had not. They said my water would be 'encouraged' to break if I had sex. Which, of course, was exactly what I wanted, someone else inside me. I did it anyway and my water did not break. They told me I would know without a doubt when the contractions began. I hadn't had any contractions that I knew of.

"Girly, now you listen to me. When are you supposed to see your doctor?"

I told her I had an appointment in a couple of hours.

"Good, you go to the doctor. And you had better not be driving yourself, Heather."

I assured her my gargantuan belly would not allow me to fit behind a steering wheel. A girlfriend was taking me.

"Good. I wish I could take you myself."

I wished that, too.

"Heather. You tell the doctor I said they need to take this baby TODAY. Isn't this your due date?"

Yes, it was.

"Good, they'll be less likely to argue with you but if they do argue, you tell them to call me."

This made me laugh.

"Don't you laugh, Heather. I AM NOT TEASING." I could picture her setting her jaw resolutely at me.

"Grandma, I don't know how to be a mother. I only know how to not be a mother."

"Now, girly, listen here. I don't know about the other fellow, I can't even say his name but I agree with Dr. Spock. You trust yourself and do not worry one bit. It will come to you, I have no doubt. Once she's born, talk to her but not that dreadful baby talk. Ooooo, I get

Never Needed Saving

so provoked when I hear people talking that way. Talk to her as if she were a human because that is what she is. As far as knowing how not to be a mother, that is a fine place to start. It will be just fine. Just let her know you will always look after her."

I asked if that was enough. She told me she believed it was. She told me that was what she had tried to do.

She was concerned about the cost of the phone call and decided I needed to rest before my appointment. She made me promise to "perk up!" We said "I love you" to each other and hung up.

I arrived at the doctor looking like a misshapen, overstuffed human marshmallow in sore need of an eyebrow pluckin'. I would not be confused with that hateful, glowing Demi Moore pregnant, naked and glorious on the cover of Vanity Fair.

In the exam room, my certified nurse midwife said "Heather, you look worn out! You been sleeping?"

No, fuck face, I have not been sleeping. I have pondered my lost faith in a loving God while I spent my nights not sleeping, peeing no more than a tablespoon of urine every 20 minutes and taking shallow breaths because I was no longer capable of taking deep ones because of small feet that I suspected, had moved from my ribs to my lungs. But sleep? No.

I shook my head no and told her I wasn't worth shooting. She gave me a hug and I began to cry. "Come on, honey, let's get you on this table."

With her assistance, I got on the table. She laid me flat on my back. I told her I would pass out from lack of

Never Needed Saving

oxygen if she didn't prop me up immediately. She did and said, all chipper and slim, "Let's take a look, shall we?"

Uh-huh, let's. After nine months of strangers being very familiar with my woman parts, my motto was "Mi vagina es su vagina." I had no shame anymore. I had told them a few months earlier they could drop the "I am now going to touch you. That is my hand on your inner thigh. I am now examining your cervix" speech. They hadn't.

"Heather, is that uncomfortable?" What your arm up to the elbow inside of me? No, it feels great.

She pulled her hand out and told me I was four centimeters dilated, my cervix was partially effaced and that I was having very strong contractions but because of the size of this creature and what must be an unusually excessive amount of amniotic fluid it probably felt like one long contraction. I had tried to tell them I would not know when I was in labor.

"That's why you haven't been sleeping! Why didn't you call us two days ago?"

I told her I was partially retarded. Then I remembered she had a child with Down's Syndrome. I stammered an apology. She helped me off the table and told me not to worry about it, she understood.

"Let's walk over to the hospital and we'll have a baby."

My doctor and midwife confabbed while I got settled. They decided I needed to rest for a few hours so they poked around in my spinal fluid and hooked me up to an epidural. My birthing instructor thought epidurals robbed the mother of the 'experience' and harmed 'the innocent child in a myriad of ways.' I thought it was the best thing since sliced bread. The next five hours gave me

Never Needed Saving

the chance to ponder how ill prepared I was to tend to a newborn human. To think about how terrified of the soft spot on her head and how I could not wait until her skull closed together. To revisit what I'd been telling my doctor for the past 4 months-that I knew in my bones, ain't no way I was going to be able to pass this child. They lied to me more. "A woman's body is an amazing thing! You'll do fine and if your perineum tears, we'll just stitch it right back up!" My mother had repeatedly informed me all my life how I'd "torn her from front to back. My asshole has never been the same. You almost killed me, Heather." She can't help it; she's just a ray of sunshine.

Around 5 p.m., John got to the hospital and the midwife came in to tell me it was time "for us to birth this baby!" Us, we. Precious. I used to like this woman. When had she turned into Mammy's more competent sister from *Gone With the Wind*? I felt the urge to punch her in the face. Pregnancy and childbirth had turned me into a wretched ogre woman.

The Pitocin drip kicked in with a vengeance and my back started to break one vertebra at a time. My water still had refused to break and I was informed they would puncture me. Fine. Once punctured, it flowed and flowed and flowed some more. "Wow! You do have an incredible amount of amniotic fluid, Heather!" Fascinating.

Push! Don't push! Breathe! Don't breathe! Push! Get on your hands and knees! Do a cartwheel! Walk down the hall briskly! At which point, mother-in-law appears with a copy of Mary Baker Eddy's Science and Health in hand. I promised God I would kill her dead if she started reading to me.

Never Needed Saving

Walk to room. Walk around room. Mother-in-law followed us in. Midwife and John helped me get back on bed.

And start barking at me again. Squat! Hang from a trapeze! Jump rope! Squat deeper! Mother-in-law starts speaking to me. I whispered a breathy, intense threat to the nurse, whose hand I was crushing: I will murder mother-in-law. I mean it. Get. Her. Out. Now.

Push! Lean! Get on your back! Do a somersault! You aren't breathing enough! On your back again! It was in this position that I heard midwife complaining of an arm cramp. I heard John say he'd take over for a while. Hi. Take over what? Midwife said "I've been holding your anus in with my thumb and now John is going to do it. Isn't that nice of him?" Yes, it was incredibly nice of him. I really appreciated it. And fucking no one mentioned to me that my anus was going to be expelled from my body. I like a heads-up on that sort of thing.

Four super fun hours came and went. I begged them to please believe me-this child was not coming out of my vagina.

"Let's get the vacuum suction pump." They did not even hear me speak words. The Oreck they used only got the top of child's head to the opening of my cervix.

"Heather, reach inside and touch her head! It will encourage your body!" No, midwife. How about you touch her head and then fuck off. I asked where the fuck John was. He said he was squatting on the floor still holding my asshole in. I thanked him. He said it was no problem.

17

Never Needed Saving

They made me touch her head. Uh-huh, I feel a large, foreign something that is not me but remains in me. Get it out or I am leaving.

I was getting irritable. Dr. Lester finally gave up and told me the child's head was too big for me to deliver vaginally. Really? She said I would have to have a c-section. I let her think it had been her idea all along. I was too tired to say I told you so.

They moved me into the operating room. I began to dry heave uncontrollably as they started disemboweling me. John gives me a play-by-play. "Your uterus is so big and weird looking. It's grey and can you feel them cutting it? Can I touch it? Want me to take a picture?" I vigorously shook my head NO and continued dry heaving. And then all of a sudden, she was born. Sound asleep. Equipped with eyes, ears, toes, fingers, nose and a thick coat of gorilla hair on her head and back. She was the most gorgeous creature I had ever seen. I knew what Kahlil Gibran meant finally when he wrote about love and knowing "the pain of too much tenderness." She took my breath away. And in spite of our close proximity to one another, we were strangers. On the way to the scale she let out a bored "Wah."

Ten pounds, one ounce. Stubborn pig-heads. I'd tried to tell them she was huge.

She was taken to get cleaned up. They put my uterus on my chest, did a couple hundred jumping jacks on it to expel all the birthing glop and sewed me back together again. Family was in town for Thanksgiving. They came in all skinny, grinning with nicely groomed eyebrows. I remember Julie, pregnant with her own first girl, holding my hand. Her smile so warm and true that I almost melted into the bed. John was off with the baby

Never Needed Saving

basking in her wondrous perfection. The morphine pump allowed me to slip in and out, from the bright, happy voices around me to the quiet darkness.

Dr. Lester came in and told me I had delivered a healthy, beautiful three-month-old girl and that my stomach would never be the same without a serious tummy tuck. "Skin can only stretch so far, you know. Yours was stretched to its capacity." No matter. Flat, toned, unscarred bellies were overrated anyhow. Look what I'd been given in exchange.

It was quiet with the family all gone home. A nurse brought Elle in from the nursery. She was hungry. The nurse asked "Do you know how to breastfeed?" Heck yes, I have worked as a wet nurse to many wealthy women! No, of course I didn't. I was banking on Elle knowing what she was doing. The nurse suggested laying her across my chest to avoid stapled incision. Lucky for me, Elle did know what she was doing. Latched right onto me. Nurse smiled and told me to buzz her when I needed to switch to other breast. I studied her peanut shaped head-grateful she seemed to be made mostly of rubber. I would've loved her even if her head stayed indented and she grew up to look like the Planter's Peanut guy. I was hypnotized by her brand new everything. Her fingernails looked recently manicured. Her jaundiced skin looked to me like a healthy tan. Her eyelashes went on for miles. I thought about just talking to her like Grandma had suggested. It did seem best to be honest with her right from the start.

So, I told her "Look, Baby, seems I am your mother and you should know I have absolutely no idea how to raise a human girl person. Even though you've been inside of me for all these months, really, we are

Never Needed Saving

strangers to each other. I promise I'll tell you the truth even when it's hard. I'll do my best to let you be who ever it is you are. If you have need of me, I will be there. I will love you forever and ever, amen, girl. Probably I am going to get this wrong but I promise I will admit it as promptly as I possibly can. I really will.

When you get older, you might hate me, I'll love you still. I promise I will look after you." An eye opened slightly and a noise came from her backside that sounded most inhuman followed by a tremendous warmth accompanied by a terrific smell. Breast milk in, breast milk out. I buzzed the nurse. She came in and removed wretched black tar from Elle's body. The nurse then placed Elle on my right breast. And together, two strangers in love, we fell asleep.

Now, almost 16 years later, Elle and I are driving home from the barn. We are more familiar with each other now. It is autumn. We have the windows down and the smell of horses in our noses mingles with the scent of fallen leaves. As we drive into the holler the road curves and a breeze blows a curtain of leaves before us and as they fall, sunlight hits them. The leaves become great pieces of golden glitter.

We both gasp, our breath taken by the vision.

We turn to each other and Elle says to me "Oh Momma! I've never seen that happen before! Have you?" I tell her I have not. We are quiet. We are no longer strangers to each other. I still don't know what I am doing. The love I feel is often all I know for sure. Grandma assured me that would be enough.

I doubted her then, but I now I believe.

Dig Cuss Sleep

No housework will be done today. The phone will go unanswered. The laundry will mildew in the washer. My family will have to scrounge their own meals. The garden calls to me. I'm off to Wonderland. A day spent in the dirt. My body works while my frets and worries vanish like bluebells after blooming.

My kids are garden orphans. They go in and out and all around me but have to repeat questions to the point of exasperation when I'm digging or pondering my next garden move. Elle and Jack are old enough now to fend for themselves while I'm gone. Bloody wounds or broken hearts are the only things powerful enough to pull me away.

My girl and boy used to come with me. As babies, they wallowed in the playpen under the shade of oak trees. They transformed into toddlers who would plant themselves naked and giddy in the grass with the water hose running until a tiny pond formed underneath their plump bottoms. Then they were old enough to ask for their own digging spot because their pie and soup recipes

Never Needed Saving

called for fresh, homemade mud. Elle needed pretty petals to decorate her earthy petit fours. Jack required a few buckets and permission to wallow like a happy piglet. Trips to plant nurseries weren't forms of torture in those days, we would lollygag up and down the aisles oohing and aahing together at all the glories held captive in black plastic pots.

They didn't care if dinner was late from lingering too long hypnotized by the colors and promises of floral splendor spinning displays of seed packets. Nowadays, my kids threaten to sic Amnesty International on me when I suggest just a real, quick trip to Pope's. One of the few things they agree on is trips to the nursery with me constitute cruel and inhumane treatment.

Elle was in a pink phase from 3 to 8 years old. She would take her Cosmos seeds and plant them in careful spirals. Marigolds and spunky zinnias called Jack's name. He would plant his deliberately at first then pour them in a pile. Jack's flower patches erupted in splats of yellow and red.

Last year, when our beloved cat Henry met his maker on Highway 95, we buried him in the garden and I watched my little boy plant marigolds on top of Henry's grave, tears drip dropped all the while as he worked. "Momma, Henry was a good garden cat. He always stayed with you and helped you plant. He was one of my very best friends and I miss him. I don't want him to be a part of everything, I want him here with us. At least his bones will stay here with us." Jack, the dogs, and our remaining cats sat for an hour at Henry's grave. When Jack had almost dehydrated himself from weeping and finally came inside. The dogs and cats stayed sleeping

Never Needed Saving

amongst the rosemary and hollyhocks, holding a lazy vigil, with Henry.

I was the gardener for an almost famous garden diva some years ago. He traveled across America and Europe for his television show while I brought his yard back from the brink of vegetative chaos. I learned precious secrets, in my favorite way, through sweet osmosis. No lectures or books, just me and his cottage garden. I trimmed his climbing roses, 'New Dawn', 'Cecille Bruner', 'Constance Spry' back to respectability. I carefully coaxed the weeds from his woodland garden so as not to disturb the wee columbine and anemone seedlings. The perennial border had been taken over by a garden thug, Buddleia (butterfly bush). I whacked the bully back so the hollyhocks and bronze fennel could stand tall as they were meant to do. His incredible collection of salvias no longer cowered under the weight of hops and morning glory vines. I chopped ten feet off of each and wove the remaining tendrils back onto the pergola where they knew they belonged. With the weight of those interloping vines off them, the salvias sprung up to show off their peacock blue blossoms.

P. wanted a "wave of violas that mimics the sky and contrasts with the green lawn". So, after he walked away, I rolled my eyes hard at his back and planted 15 flats of violas, "blues, whites and purples only, please Heather", in the front of his reclaimed border. In his garden shed, I became intimately acquainted with 20 varieties of amaryllis, 7 varieties of hyacinths. I potted up hundreds for an early spring T.V. shoot. All the while, I wondered how P. could have his bit of earth, like Mary in The Secret Garden desired, and not work it himself. The

Never Needed Saving

quest for fame and fortune gobbled up all of P.'s attention and energy.

Gardens, like children, cannot hide a lack of love and tender care.

I made the mistake of watching his show a few months after planting 1500 tulip and 2500 narcissi bulbs in P.'s formal round garden. I'd spent days digging, setting and tucking in those 4000 papery wonders. And there he was telling how after the Thanksgiving meal, he and his merry family went out and planted the thousands of bulbs together in the remainders of the idyllic holiday afternoon. My ego couldn't take it.

Pissed me right off, him taking all the credit. I knew how Martha Stewart's people must feel. I don't trust people who claim to be gardeners but never have dirt stuck under their fingernails.

But P. didn't have the memories of the digging I had. Like the one of Elle lollygagging over my head in the limbs of his crabapple tree, coming down only for another spoonful of honey from the jar sitting on a garden bench, and the halcyon autumn sunlight and the heady smell of moist, rich earth cocooned around me while I buried all those bulbs.

I've read hundreds of gardening books. Their precise designs whirl around in my head. The strict rules and solemn warnings given by professional plantsmen and women are temporarily accepted as gospel. But once out in Eden, the edicts of learned minds fall away. Sometimes petal, root, soil, leaf and trunk whisper to me. I don't tell serious gardeners my great wish, to have gardens that would make hobbits proud and bewitching enough for fairies to live in.

Never Needed Saving

These days, plants have to be largely self-sufficient to be installed in my yard as I'm not inclined to tolerate the demands of high maintenance hybrid bitches, except, of course, for the one I married and the two I gave birth to. I've made exceptions for some in the garden, like bluebells and peonies, only because once, if they deign to establish themselves, they require little more than admiration. But they had to sit through a serious talking-to before I planted them in the spot which best met their needs. I loved them while I dug the holes, threatened them with eternity spent in the compost pile while pulling the pot away from their cramped roots and went back to tender as I gathered and tucked them into the ground.

The only roses I allow are heirloom varieties like 'Old Blush' and 'The Fairy'. When these easy care glories slice and dice me to a bloody mess I yell "Fuck off you little bitches! Why do I put up with you?" They roll their pink petals at me the way my children roll their eyes when I fuss at them. I'm not to be taken seriously. The roses know what my children know, I couldn't bear to be without them. So when the gardening day is done, I walk inside. The house is still dirty, the answering machine is blinking. I start the mildewy load of laundry again. The family didn't starve. I lie in bed bone-tired, mind calm and easy with the smell of dirt stuck in my nose. And the garden, for now, is satisfied. As I drift off to sleep, I know there are bewitched fairies creeping in the moonlight to my bit of earth, and if there were hobbits in Greenback they would be proud to call this garden their own.

"Are you making Magic?" he asked sharply.
Dickon's curly mouth spread in a cheerful grin.

Never Needed Saving

"*Tha's doin' Magic thysel'*" he said. "*It's same Magic as made these 'ere work out o' th' earth*" and he touched with his thick boot a clump of crocuses in the grass. Colin looked down at them.

"*Aye,*" he said slowly, "*there couldna' be bigger Magic than that there—there couldna' be.*"

The Secret Garden
Frances Hodgson Burnett

Counting Crows

    The left foot, right foot, breathe in, breathe out of walking is the closest I get to purposeful meditation. I've read that daydreaming, going off to Wonderland, is a form of meditation, but for me, at least, it is not purposeful--just a gift from some unknown grace I am happy to receive throughout my days.

    I follow my faithful companion, Edward the gentleman collie, on this wooded trail. He is calm and true. He prefers to keep three or four paces ahead of me. Our paces synchronize beautifully, with no conscious effort. We match steps as if by magic. We glide through the ankle-deep leaves on Ridgetop Loop Trail at Ft. Loudoun State Park, each step we take rustling up peace. The heady smell of fallen leaves is intoxicating. A group of crows in the treetops above are cawing, holding a midday meeting. A flock of crows is called a 'murder', the folk legend says, because a group will sometimes kill a dying crow. Maybe it's just because it sounds like a murder is in progress when the crows gather and they're somehow in on it. Would other crows actually kill a dying crow? And if they would, does this mean they'd do it to end suffering? Are they capable of mercy?

Counting crows to predict the future:

One is for sorrow.

Two is for joy.

Three for a letter.

Four or a boy.

Five for silver.

Six for gold.

Seven for a story that's never been told.

I count eight. What does this mean? Maybe it's something only crows know.

My bones tell me we can depend too much on such things as counting crows or believing crows practice mercy killing to figure out what will happen next in our lives. I only know that the older I get, the younger I feel and the less I am sure of all that I once thought was written in stone.

I understand now what once mystified me--if you meet the Buddha on the road, kill him. There is no One Big Answer. Anymore, I do not desire a final answer, I am happy with the merrily, merrily down the stream of life. In the woods, in the mountains, at the ocean, in the desert I feel the Great Big Everything in a way that I do not inside manmade walls. I read once, that not knowing meant one was teachable. I am teachable these days.

I grew up in a lovely church. I met my dearest and oldest friend Leah in those walls. I gathered love and a desire to serve from my days in those manmade walls. I was given a sense of Love, big sweet and true from the

Never Needed Saving

years in those walls. Forever and ever, Amen will I be grateful for those precious days. Took me until I was 30 to understand those walls were in need, for me, of bursting out of. Now, I try to make wherever I happen to be my catholic church. The Catholics were smart to use that word meaning "universal" to name their religion. With the small "c," catholic also means eclectic. Tolerant. Broad-minded. I am sure they prefer the definition of universal to the other definitions. Those souls who are near me, they are my living altars. And how I worship on bended knee with bowed head and eyes closed at those adored altars. They are all holy relics to me. The ones I love are Alpha and Omega, stardust and ash, past, present and future Buddhas to me. Sometimes I fear I will burst at their loveliness, their holy brilliance. It is more than one heart can hold. They have no idea of how wonderful they all are. Or maybe they do. I hope they know, each and every one. There is a Patty Griffin song that says:

> Cause you can't make somebody see
>
> By the simple words you say
>
> All their beauty from within
>
> Sometimes, they just look away.

If only they could see what I see, what I feel, what I know, when I am on bended knee at their altar. The beauty, the love, the wonder of them leaves me breathless, they fill me up to bursting, and this cup of mine runneth over with the glory of them.

Shades of brown, rust, darker brown, and grey are interrupted by gangly splats of green Christmas ferns. I smile when I notice their carefree fronds lollygagging over top of leaves released from trees for the greater good. Trees let go and fret not about their loss of foliage. New foliage will come, in time. No tears are shed. No funerals held. A natural acceptance and forward movement. I am granted comfort and courage from these walks I take in the woods. Edward does not take these gifts for granted. He does not thinkthinkthink about how and why and when, rather he knows. From him, too, I learn to breathe, listen, watch. I learn to be like him. To just be. His tail wags enough to let me know he is well pleased with his current circumstance. Occasionally, he looks back at me. I talk to him. His tail acknowledges my voice, my musings with more enthusiastic wagging, and I swear, a sparkle in his eyes. Edward stands sentinel and is patient when I stop to write down a phrase or a feeling, a plant name. I thank him for his patience and on we go.

Maybe God is a giant asshole with an inferiority complex demanding adherence to strict rules. Maybe He needs that to feel like a real deity. Maybe I'll be in serious everlasting trouble when my heart stops, when I breathe no more, when this life of mine is over. Maybe I will reap a horrible harvest for this life spent wondering and wandering. Maybe my disregard for arcane rules will be met with severe repercussions. I will accept those consequences. I would not trade one moment spent in this wanderlust, this adoration of those I've had the pleasure of knowing, this unruliness inside of me which feels, often, unladylike and just right all at the very same time. I'll take even the 68 levels of Vietnamese Buddhist Hell that my cousin Sarah told me about which include the Naraka (or purgatory) of Nirarbuda. The "burst blister" Naraka. Himalayan cold seems like American South summer to this cold. Blisters erupt and ooze for 20 times longer than it would take to "empty a barrel of sesame seeds if one took one seed out every hundred

Never Needed Saving

years." Yes, those who I love are worth this punishment. That is how precious you are, how remarkable, how wonderful and glorious each of you are to me.

Maybe I am a fool.

But I do not think so.

Deep down, I feel the Alpha and Omega is vast enough for us all. Could be wishful, hopeful thinking, I'll allow that, only it seems silly to think we must all fit into a tiny box. A Christian box. A Jewish box. A Buddhist box. A Muslim box. A Hindu box. A Zen box. A Roman Catholic box. A Pagan box. Surely, the Great Big Everything allows for more than a handful of ways back. If not, I'll stand corrected and accept my just desserts.

Edward and I head into the newly opened Lost Shoe Trail, an extension of the Meadow Loop Trail. We enter a quiet, young, pine wood which soon gives way to a meadow of heavenly proportions. The grasses are shoulder high. Cedars and dogwoods make islands of shade in the openness. I convince Edward to go within the grasses. Last time, I had beef jerky to aid my argument. This time, all I have is my voice. He obliges. A lovely dog, and most agreeable.

Now, we are almost hidden in the grasses. I lie down. Edward stands careful guard. I stare at the sky, cloudless, November crisp blue sky.

Never Needed Saving

Goodbye to Uncle Tom

His good byes were said, his affairs were in order when the quiet took him. Uncle Tom lingered between here and there with the remnants of a well-lived life warming up the cold hospital room. A collage of snapshots filled the wall facing the bed, the blue boiled wool beret to replace the hair the chemo had taken hung on the back of a chair. The quilt Aunt Ann had made from his old flannel shirts was tucked oh so gently around his emaciated body. Trivial Pursuit, two decks of cards, and books filled the windowsill. A metal bucket filled with laminated smiling lips taped to dowels waited like party favors on the bedside table. His youngest child and only daughter, Sarah had made them so she could turn her goddamned frown upside down.

The summons went out to my legion of loud and rowdy kin strewn all over the map that it was Time. We gathered at Aunt Ann and Uncle Tom's house and hugged, kissed, wept and regressed. From there, we went in groups of 3 or 4 to the hospital rotating like factory workers to watch over Uncle Tom. We went on faith that he could hear us talk of his favorite things: sailing, South

Never Needed Saving

Carolina peaches, Edisto Island in May, boiled peanuts and old-fashioned grits, hikes in the Rockies. We promised to look after Aunt Ann and his 3 grown children. We brought bottles of Dr. Pepper, kept the TV on The Weather Channel, and caressed his wax paper hands with almond scented lotion that for a moment would distract us from the dying smell enveloping him slowly each day. We told him how, in one way or another, he had saved each and every one of us. No doubt, our displays were worse than the cancer for this quiet, prudent, modest man.

We reconvened in Aunt Ann's kitchen on the 6th day of waiting. Michael, the eldest, once a wild child had become calm and stoic, much like his father, stood near his mother. Despite his deep sadness, he emanated a tranquility. Aunt Ann told us his wish to donate his organs would be unfulfilled because the cancer had rendered all but his retinas unusable. David, his middle child, mentioned dryly that he'd been ogling his dad's retinas for years and we heehawed until our bellies ached. Aunt Ann told us how during the meeting with the unctuous funeral director, David had completely unnerved the man by saying "We have plans to scatter Dad all over Hell and Creation. Should we bring a couple of logs to throw in with the body so we have enough Dad to spread around?" Where I come from irreverence is like gravy, there ain't no such thing as too much.

Later on that evening, the morphine drip that kept him unconscious and out of pain, seemed to stop working. Low, ragged moans came from this once composed man who now looked like some enormous, wretched nestling who had been flash frozen. His hands were like talons locked in an unnatural attempt to perch.

Never Needed Saving

When asked how long Uncle Tom would be trapped in his wasting, failing body, a doctor said God and Tom were working out the details and when they were satisfied, he would go on.

After days of Kansas City's sub-zero temperatures and gloomy grey skies, January 18th saw the sun come back accompanied by a crisp, winter blue sky. We were drinking coffee and eating fried grits when the call came. We heard Aunt Ann say "Okay, we'll be right there." Her smile was true and the tears that slid down her face were sweet relief and instant loneliness. "Tom is gone. You are now to refer to me as 'The Widow Wedaman'. Tom told me a few weeks ago I'd earned a title." She said she thought he would have gone sooner but we wouldn't leave him alone. We kept hovering and running our mouths. He snuck off to Glory before we could get back to the hospital. Good for him.

I remember, Uncle Tom, the time you and Aunt Ann, on your way to Montreat, NC, stopped for a visit here in Greenback. I remember standing with you at the edge of my vegetable garden. We were quiet, admiring the okra before we walked in to do some pickin'. I remember how being near you always eased me. How watching you through the years, I learned how there was no need to thrash about, wallow in troubles, gnash my teeth. The quote from A.A. Milne "Rivers know this. There is no hurry. We shall get there someday." Reminds me of you, Uncle Tom. I wonder if where you are you remember that day in Greenback. I do. I remember. It is one of my favorite memories and it was with you.

Never Needed Saving

Never Needed Saving

Sarah Heartburn Runs Away

Momma taught me to read when I was four. She ordered I Can Read books, which came once a month, in a box just for me. It was a little Christmas every month. I was sitting on her lap the first time I read a book all by myself. It was called Danny and the Dinosaur. She was proud of me. She hugged and kissed me and told me I was the smartest, best girl she knew. Back then, my momma loved me so much.

I knew good girls did not run away from their mothers and that by leaving my mother, I would never be good again. I also knew I was going anyway. For a week, I planned my secret escape. Only treasures would go with me. I felt certain I would never be allowed to enter Momma's house again after she discovered me gone, so I chose as wisely as I could. Pieces of quartz chipped off the boulder in the backyard, the gold signet ring that was Grandma's when she was a girl, a turtle shell in mint condition found in the big woods bordering our neighborhood, slate gathered from the creek at the bottom of the woods and books. I loved all my books.

Never Needed Saving

They were all my favorites, but I only had room for the most precious ones.

Charlotte's Web, *Stuart Little*, *The Trumpet of the Swan*. These went in my backpack first. Grandma had given me these. There was an inscription, written in her precise script, inside the cover of each one.

The Trumpet of the Swan read:

> Happy Vacation 1977!
>
> May 31, 1977

Charlotte's Web:

> August 16, 1974
>
> Six years old!

Stuart Little:

> Heather, remember you are as brave as Stuart.
>
> Thinking of you with love.

I packed a couple of books I considered, with a decade's wisdom, to be 'baby' books. Aunt June wrote in *William's Doll*:

> August 1976
>
> Heather, this is one of my favorite books! I hope you love it as much as I did. Read it to Grainger so he can be as good a Daddy as yours.
>
> Love, Love, Love!
>
> Aunt June

I had done as Aunt June hoped and read it to my little brother. I worried if I didn't, he might turn out to be a bad Daddy when he was grown.

Never Needed Saving

The inscription in *I Like Butterflies* read:

For broken-arm days

March 13, 1976

From Grandma and Granddaddy

The *Little House on the Prairie* books were from Aunt Ann. I had read them all twice, but couldn't bear to separate the set. The same mentality forced me to bring all of *The Chronicles of Narnia*. I packed these books with the hope they would remind me that I had once been a good girl well loved by her momma.

Another bag was required and enabled me to bring a small, cedar treasure box Daddy had gotten for me in Mountain Home, Arkansas, the time we went camping in the Ozarks. In the box, I kept found feathers, the sterling baby rattle from Grandma given when I was born, my Barry Manilow fan club card and the ticket stubs from Barry's concert and Jesus Christ Superstar! I only allowed myself to open it occasionally in hopes the cedar smell would last almost forever.

Some snapshots of good times gone by went in, too, but only three of the dolls Grandma had brought back from her travels would fit. I chose the dolls from Thailand because the traditional Thai dresses they wore had tiny sequins that sparkled when I held them in the light.

I picked my favorite pair of jeans for my journey. The ones with the rainbow stitched up one leg and down the other. I wore my Earth shoes because the thick, rubber soles made me fall as a 12-year old, and my Cal Ledbetter for Congress t-shirt because it made me feel just a little bit famous even though my uncle lost the election.

Never Needed Saving

When the packing was finished, I put the bags in the way back of my closet. Momma rarely looked in there. Grainger caught me as I attempted to camouflage the bags with some dirty clothes just in case Momma did look. I had not planned to tell my 7-year old brother about running away. I was going to trick him into leaving the only home he'd ever known. After a promise to not tell and a bribe of $1.00, in quarters, as Grainger demanded, I told him why I was leaving. She was not the momma she used to be. She was crazy. She was mean. She was almost always drunk. And anymore, she hated me. Grainger agreed Momma was always mad at me. Not mad at him and he did infinitely more stupid things than I did. He didn't understand why. But I did.

One night, a few weeks before I made my decision, I had heard her crying in the kitchen. I'd tiptoed out of my bedroom and leaned in the hallway listening to her sob. After a minute or two, I stepped into the light of the kitchen. She had turned and barked at me "What the hell do you want, Heather?" I asked why she was so sad. I asked if she needed a hug.

"Not from you I don't. You are the last person I want a hug from."

I struggled to keep the tears in my eyes but failed. They fell down my miserable face. The lump in my throat would not be dismissed by swallows. I heard myself whisper "Oh. Okay, Momma."

"Don't you want to know why? You just gonna stand there-feeling sorry for yourself?"

I told her I didn't know what she wanted me to say. I moved to the wall and slid down to the cold, linoleum floor. And she told me why.

Never Needed Saving

She told me when I was a baby, I had cried and cried when she held me. Daddy would take me and I would stop for him. Grandma would take me from her and I would stop for her, too. She told me I was theirs, I had never been hers. That I had never loved her the way I should. She told me she never had understood me and didn't like the way I looked at her with my big "cow eyes". That every time she looked at me, all she saw was Williams. And she hated The Williams. She did not want any part of them. They never had understood her. They said she was crazy.

She had crouched down in front of me and growled, "You think I don't know I'm crazy? I know."

She dared me to be honest, admit to her face that I did not love her.

Only I did love her. I wanted to save her but finally saw that I could not. She seemed to feel better and I felt covered in her corrosive, verbal poisons.

"Quit cryin' and go to bed."

I stood up and sobbed my little self back to bed. I willed my heart to turn to stone, impenetrable granite but it would not oblige me. I clenched my teeth and tried to not absorb her venom. Again, failure. I was full up with her crazy hate and had a soft chalk heart smashed to smithereens.

The next day, Momma acted like nothing had happened. She didn't seem to remember what she'd said to me. But I remembered.

Grainger said she was still nice to him. He wasn't mad at me. He understood and if she was as mean to him he probably would run away from her, too. But, Momma still loved him, so he was probably staying put. He

Never Needed Saving

wanted to know who, besides me, he would have to play with if he changed his mind. If Randy Alexander could run away with us, then Grainger would go. I despised Randy. He would call the house and yell in my ear: "Where's Grainger? This is Randy. R-A-N-D-Y from next door. Tell him to come over NOW! I have a good idea. Don't forget! R-A-N-D-Y!" I knew how to spell his stupid name. I hated him. His idea of a good day was getting my brother to drink bleach or tying him up to the fire hydrant wearing only his underwear with 3 miles of fishing line or fashioning bed sheets into capes a la Superman and encouraging Grainger to jump from the top of our stairs over and over until his teeth came through his bottom lip. All of Grainger's Emergency Room visits were Randy-related. I loved my brother but he was an idiot with poor taste in friends. I could not bear the thought of the long walk to Daddy's house with Randy. What if we ended up hobos and had to ride the rails until we were grown-ups?

Uh-uh. No way. I told Grainger his friend was forbidden to runaway with us. Fine, he said, I'm staying here. He would, however, keep my secret and help me on the day I left so Momma wouldn't know I was gone until I had gotten a good head start.

Through muffled sobs, I wrote my note to Momma. I wanted to beg her to stop being crazy, convince her to stop drinking so much vodka, to care about my ballet classes enough to wash my leotard and tights. I wanted to tell her how I missed the olden days. The days forever ago, when before school I would wait for breakfast on top of the heating vent in the kitchen wearing my flannel nightgown that made me feel like Laura Ingalls. The hot air would surround me and I

Never Needed Saving

would watch her drink her coffee. I wanted to let her know how I was torn in two, the ache in my heart felt like it was killing me a little bit every day. Scream that she had torn me all asunder and why would she ever want to do that? I wanted to promise that I would be a good girl and be home on time from playing in the woods with Jessica instead of always being late. I wanted to tell her how sorry I was for knocking stuff off the kitchen counter all the time and being so afraid at the doctor's office it took three grown ups to hold me down for shots and stitches. I wanted to swear I would never humiliate her again by being the only kid who got so scared at Charlotte's Halloween party she was called to come get me immediately. I would be a brave girl, no longer terrified of vampires, needles or vomiting. I wanted her to know I was hers, too and if she'd let me, I'd try real, real hard not to look so Williams-y. I wanted her to know how much I missed reading stories with her.

But I didn't. I knew it would only make her more mad, more sad. Instead, I wrote:

Please Do NOT Disturb!!!!!

I am reading until 5:30 pm!!!

I told her how I loved her so much and always would. I often left notes like this on my door. She would suspect nothing. She would think I was being melodramatic and holler for me around 5:30. "Oh, Sarah Heartburn! Come out of your reading cave and get ready for dinner." I hated being called Sarah Heartburn. And Grandma said I wasn't melodramatic. She said I just felt things very deeply. So, there, Momma.

The runaway day arrived. I begged Grainger to please, please come with me. He refused, again. He

Never Needed Saving

didn't understand I was crossing the line from good to bad. If I left without him, I would probably be forever lost to the darkness where wretched girls had to go and live alone, without the no-matter-what kind of love. Only the worst sort of girl left her little brother behind. My desperation was lost on him. He told me to hurry up because he and Randy were going to spend the day looking for dead stuff to bury in our backyard so they could make their very own cemetery. If I got to Daddy's, he'd see me next weekend. He let me hug him tight. I taped the note to my bedroom door and closed it tight.

My look-out told me the coast was clear. I stood weighted down with my treasures at the top of the basement stairs. We looked at each other for a minute then he told me to hurry up already! I was cutting into his dead stuff gathering time. I went down the stairs and out the door, into the backyard. I walked into the alley where my first cat, Fluffy, had been murdered by the neighbor's German Shepherd two years earlier. I did not look back. My eyes threatened to overflow, so I had to lean my head back to keep the tears from falling. A crying girl with two bulging bags was bound to arouse suspicions. I'd read enough Nancy Drew to know about suspicious behavior. I did not let my tears fall until I had walked two blocks crossing Elm Street back into the safety of another alley.

I hoped Daddy would not be mad at me for running away to him. I hoped he would let me live with him. I hoped he would look after me. Inside the bag on my left shoulder, I had my copy of A Little Princess. Inside the cover was written:

For Heather

From Daddy

Never Needed Saving

Dallas, Texas

June 18, 1976

He'd gone on a business trip and brought the book as proof he'd been thinking of me while he was gone. When I read the inscription, my feelings were hurt. No "I love you." After I read it, I realized my daddy loved me as much as the daddy in the story loved his girl. He did not have to say "I love you," the whole story told me he did. I'd read the book twice. I felt certain enough to keep walking towards Daddy's house.

And still. Every step I took, a little more goodness seemed to slip away. Only I couldn't, wouldn't stop and turn around. It felt too late. Momma and I had become strangers to each other. I felt all alone. None of the books prepared me for the feeling of being so disconnected. It seemed as if I followed behind my body like I was a shadow girl. And I hoped the treasures carried on my shoulders would be enough to conjure up memories of the real, good girl I had once been.

About the Author

Before adding her unique and earthy voice to the pantheon of great American writers, Heather Leigh Williams spent an itinerant life in that Gothic wonderland, that literary forge, that greatest of all muses, the American South.

Ms. Williams worked every job from hammering exquisite grails in stately Charleston, South Carolina, to keeping the garden of a renowned Master of Natural Beauty in Little Rock, Arkansas, to listening to people talk a lot about pulling dents in Jacksonville, Florida. No work was too dirty for this hands-on, grade-A daughter of toil. Everything just added up to more detail – and thus truth – in her art. And how we now benefit from her lonely labors!

Nowadays Ms. Williams calls the humid hollers of Greenback, Tennessee home, and her passions propel through tree-sized, variegated liriope the muscular flanks of Sassy the Quarter Horse, who sadly does not descend from that most famous stallion, the Tennessee Stud. Ms. Williams does what she can to pass on her grandmother's absolute love to two wondrously fine children and to other like-minded people of checkered past and lesser worth who pass her door. Look for the house enveloped in a modern-day Eden and you'll know where you are. That's where we found her.

Today Ms. Williams is hard at work on her next book, a further development of the magical story included in this anthology, "Sarah Heartburn Runs Away." We all look forward to a classic coming-of-age story detailing the flight of 8-year old Sarah from her unhappy dome and her redemption through the transmogrification of literature, that all-purifying catalyst, marketed to the young adult ladyhood segment.

Electronic correspondence can be directed to Ms. Williams through her publishing agents:

>Ms. Heather Leigh Williams
>
>c/o Least Shining Crescent Press
>
>leastshiningcrescent@gmail.com

Never Needed Saving

Also from Least Shining Crescent Press

www.leastshiningcrescent.com

My Last Name is Volcano

Leah and Isaac Wedaman

337 pages

$17.78 print

$1.25 eBook

A spunky "quotumentary," or compilation of hilarious, meaningful, and true, context-free quotations from two thinkers of the new generation. Topics include transportation, gender, mass media, animals, the imagination, relationships, opinions, aggression.

Highest praise for **My Last Name Is Volcano**!

Ever ask yourself questions like the following (now, be honest!):
> What happens when a storm blows off a tire?
> What does Aunt Sarah do with the chocolate?
> Do birds grow?
> Who is my running konkadoodle?

Well, now you have the wonderfully hilarious answers, right in the palm of your hand!

Yes, this six-by-nine-inch tome contains within it over 300 amazing and rib-crackingly funny quotations from a pair of America's "new generation" of thinkers. Quotations that can be memorized and applied successfully in a variety of contexts.

Join hundreds of other satisfied readers by treating yourself to one of life's pleasures (this book), and soon you will yell out loud, tears streaming down your cheeks, what everyone else on the block already has: "My last name is Volcano, too!"

www.ingramcontent.com/pod-product-compliance
Lightning Source LLC
Chambersburg PA
CBHW022344040426
42449CB00006B/717